# Intermediate Guide to Punch Needle

# Table of Contents

# Introduction

Needle punching is one of today's most popular crafts. Whether you are looking for a leisure pursuit, a pleasant way to earn extra income, or interested in investing in a thriving business, you are in the right place. This is the second part of the book in the series that deals with needle punching. Part 1 of the series, entitled *Punch Needle for Beginners*, deals with simple everyday designs. The beginners' book is right for you if you want to learn the basic skills required to make designs with colorful yarn loops on loosely woven fabric, specifically chosen for the purpose. Part II of the series is an intermediate guide that expands your skillset with slightly more challenging designs and techniques, all accompanied by detailed and descriptive explanations.

Punch needle embroidery is similar to rug hooking. In punch needle embroidery, you do not have to stitch through the fabric. Instead, you utilize the punch needle to punch the thread into the fabric while the needle still stays on the surface. Needle punching is far simpler than regular embroidery. You can quickly and gracefully create all kinds of craft projects, from simple objects to complex landscapes and portraits, by learning this unique embroidery technique.

This book provides a descriptive account of how to select the right materials for your project, including choosing different size yarns or punching both stiff and smooth fabrics using a variety of frames. You get access to several needle punching and rug hooking projects that allow you to acquire a new skill every time. As part of your learning experiences, the book contains several walkthroughs of selected projects. As you go along, you will get introduced to complex projects and new skills you may be able to apply to your creative projects. By the time you reach the end of the book, you will find yourself equipped with a unique skill-set to pursue any needle punching or rug hooking project from basic to intermediate level. Beyond this basic skill-set, you will also feel confident about starting and managing your online store through leading platforms such as Etsy. So look no further, and let's start needle punching.

# Chapter One:
## Needle Punching and Rug Hooking - Recollecting Background and Basics

The practice of punching a needle through the fabric with yarn attached to it is an ancient art. The origin of the art is not certain, although people have traced the beginning of punch needle embroidery to ancient Egypt when the artwork became quite prominent. Others believe that the technique may have begun in Medieval Europe, and the most commonly cited places of its origin are Russia, Britain, or Germany. Sometimes, specific forms of art may be attributed to their place of origin. In the USA, Russian punch needlework is quite popular and features extremely fine thread.

Historians believe that the punch needle craft dates back to the 15th Century when people referred to the art form by the name "punch stitch." In ancient times, artisans typically used the punch needle to create beautiful rugs. They also decorated religious attire using punch needle embroidery when men sailed across the sea.

The punch needle may sometimes be referred to as "punch needle rug hooking." Loops created from the punch needle embroidery technique impart a carpet-like look and feel. The loops may be tightly punched into the fabric, or longer loops may be cut to impart a different kind of appearance. Other terms may also be used to describe the art form, such as "thread painting" to indicate the scenes that are depicted in the finished piece, similar to an oil painting. Other terms used to refer to the art are "Bunka," "Punch needle embroidery," "Russian embroidery," "Punch embroidery," or simply "Punch."

There are two types of punch needle crafts that most artisans practice. The first one is the "rug hooking" skill that utilizes a large gauge hooking tool and yarn. The other type of punch needle embroidery is one that utilizes embroidery floss along with a thinner needle. Punch needle embroidery fabric has a loose weaving, unlike a regular fabric. All you need for punch needle embroidery is the fabric meant for the purpose, a good quality yarn, and the punch needle tool.

Finished pieces of punch needle crafts may look very different from one another, although they use the same technique. Most embroidered pieces are yarn crafts, and some appear to be embroidery floss. The type of yarn used in embroidery determines its final look and feel. For example, artisans may use either lusters, polyester yarns, or acrylic yarns to achieve a delicate piece of artwork.

The process of creating beautiful embroidery designs is quite simple. You just thread the needle with the yarn you selected and pierce the needle into the fabric. Then you pull out the needle to create a loop. You keep going this way, creating loops, until you have achieved a part of your design in a specific color. You may continue looping through the motif, changing the yarn whenever you require a new color or a different effect.

The key to achieving a flawless piece of embroidery is mastering the loops. You want to create tight loops, so that the loops hold the loose fabric together. This is the essential technique you need to master to achieve a finished piece that does not fall apart. Unlike traditional embroidery, where you would tie a knot on the reverse side to prevent your yarn or thread from coming off, the punch needle does not make use of any knots. The key takeaway here is that making light and quick loops requires the most practice and mastery.

There are several reasons why you may want to go for punch needle embroidery rather than any other form of art. First, it is one of the simplest forms of thread work and may be accomplished with simple tools. The basic skills can be learned in a few hours.

Furthermore, whether you are a novice or experienced fabric artist, you enjoy the flexibility to select either side of your finished work to create your final masterpiece. While one side creates a design with hooks, the other side builds an image using loops. At the end of your project, you have a choice to switch between the two representations.

Moreover, punch needle embroidery requires very few supplies, even for detailed projects. The only tools you need are your punch needle, yarn, and piece of cloth. It does not require a lot of storage space and is quite easy to carry around.

Once you have developed a good level of expertise in looping your way through fabric, you are all set to create anything from rugs to pillow covers, purses, wall hangings, and even stuffed toys!

**Chapter Summary**

- Needle punching is an ancient art, tracing its origin to Europe, Egypt, Russia, Britain, and even Germany.

- Needle punching is mainly associated with rugs.

- Several terms have been used to refer to needle punching and rug hooking, including "thread painting," "Bunka," "Punch needle embroidery," "Punch," and "Punch embroidery."

- In rug hooking, you typically use a large gauge hook and thick yarn, whereas, in needle punching, a thin needle and embroidery floss is a typical choice.

- Needle punching provides you the flexibility to create many different types of patterns and effects in your craftwork.

- The way to proceed with needle punching is to simply thread a needle and pierce it in the fabric to make loops.

- Most people choose to pursue needle punching because of its simplicity.

- You can create a variety of projects, including purses, pillow covers, stuffed toys, and wall hangings.

- The only materials you would need, even for the most complex projects, are the punch needle, a piece of fabric, a frame to hold the fabric, and yarn.

- You could use either side of your finished artwork for your final display.

In the next chapter, you will recollect a basic description of materials required for any needle punching project. You already have a good grasp of the materials needed for punch needle projects. The next chapter builds upon that knowledge and lists the pros and cons of different materials. It serves as a good starting point to gather in-depth information on different materials available in the market and make prudent choices when collecting supplies for your projects.

# Chapter Two: Materials for Needle Punching Projects - Pros, Cons, and Quick Tips

You are already familiar with the materials required for needle punching projects. A quick reference is included below:

- Foundation fabric (such as monk's cloth) - Your loose weave fabric that serves as a backing for your pattern

- Your choice of yarn - You will need yarn to make loops on the fabric

- The punch needle - This is the tool to punch the yarn through the fabric

- Embroidery frame - A frame to fix the fabric and keep it taut throughout your needle punching activity

- Your chosen pattern or design - You will transfer this design to the fabric to complete your project

- Pencil or erasable marker - You will need this if you are drawing the pattern on your fabric

- Scissors - To cut the fabric or yarn and finish up with your project

It's now time to go a bit more in detail to understand how the different materials complement each other. You want to be able to discern between the qualities of these tools and supplies and choose a combination that is most suitable for your project.

***The Punch Needle*** - As you may understand, a punch needle is a tool that makes loops through the fabric when you thread yarn into it. When working with the punch needle, you may be using either yarn, or ribbon, or floss to work your way through the fabric meant for the purpose. Punch needles may be available in different sizes. For example, common punch needles may have different measurements such as 1.3mm, 1.6mm, or 2.2mm in terms of length. Its threader may measure 18 cm. Finally, the punch needle comes with a handle that is 11 cm long and 1.5cm wide. Punch needles are available from many different brands. When selecting a punch needle for your project, there are several aspects of the tool you may want to consider.

Punch needles typically come in two different sizes - the smaller size is used with embroidery floss, and the larger size is used with the rug yarn. It is typically your preference that matters when choosing the punch needle that is most suitable. The smaller needle works best with weavers cloth or linen to achieve a tight weave. On the other hand, larger needles that work with wool yarns are most effective on fabrics that have a loose weaving, such as primitive linen, monk's cloth, rug warp, or burlap.

**<u>Adjustable punch needle pros and cons</u>** - The adjustable punch needle has a unique threading system. It is widely preferred as it can create many loops of different lengths. Some offer as many as six different lengths of loops. The other characteristic that makes a punch needle better than others is its construction. A stainless steel needle with a wooden handle provides a comfortable grip to be able to complete even complex and time-consuming projects. A significant aspect of selecting the right punch needle is how swiftly and smoothly it goes in and comes out of the fabric. High-quality stainless steel needles tend to provide the best performance as you get a smooth rhythmic up and down motion while working with them.

Another important feature of the adjustable handle punch needle is that the tool contains a hollow needle without an open slot. This means that the yarn always tends to stay in the needle without you having to worry about rethreading it during your embroidery. The needle alleviates common problems such as the yarn falling off from the needle while you are still working on your project, or the yarn getting stuck or pulled off in the middle of your pursuit.

Some people may find it difficult to work with an adjustable handle punch needle as it does not extend across the full length of the hand. They may prefer to go with another model that may not offer as many advantages but still fits the hand well. However, an aspect that might sometimes limit its popularity is the requirement of a threader to be able to get the yarn along its path. This means that you have to carry the accompanying threader, making it cumbersome and inconvenient.

**<u>Oxford Punch Needle</u>** - The Oxford punch needle has a large handle and is popular among fabric artists. The primary factor that sets it apart from others is its ergonomic design. In terms of performance, it's very similar to the adjustable punch needle and allows you to achieve a rhythmic pierce-and-retract activity. It's quite easy to thread and has a sturdy construction. However, it does not allow you to punch more than a single size of the loop, somewhat limiting your creativity.

**<u>Craftsman punch needle</u>** - The Craftsman punch has an easy threading mechanism and allows many different lengths of loops. Its complex threading mechanism with a locking system is its biggest disadvantage, and so is the fact that it may require frequent rethreading.

**<u>Ultra punch needle</u>** - The Ultra punch needle features an ergonomic design and comes with different-size needle tips. You will most commonly find it with a fine, medium, and large tip. It allows adjustable loops and works with fine yarn or embroidery floss (3-6 strands). It has limited utility as it does not support the use of thick yarn. It also requires a threader, which is more of an inconvenience for the fabric artist on-the-go.

**<u>Factors that influence your buy decision</u>** - Several other types of punch needles are available in the market, and function very differently. Customers generally prefer those that do not require a threader, have an ergonomic design, and move swiftly through the fabric.

Needles offer a single length of the loop of varying lengths, and you may want to select a needle that meets your requirements. Sometimes, you may decide to have different loop lengths for your project and end up buying several needles, which translates to a higher cost. Therefore, it is best to decide the loop length that you are likely to work with just before beginning the project.

The material used for constructing the needle may also make a difference in certain cases. Punch needles may be made from plastic or copper. Hard plastic needles are generally sturdy. There may be other materials used to construct the needle as well, and you want to get a feel of the needle before purchasing it. If you have prior experience, you may also want to make a quick online purchase and get started with your chosen project.

The most important aspect of a punch needle is concerning its performance. Certain punch needles catch fabric as you work with your project, and may not be smooth during the punching action. These flaws may take away rhythm from the artwork. In many cases, there may be flaws with the construction itself, and the needle may pop out of its container, which most artisans would not prefer. It's best to settle for a reputable brand to achieve not just a tidy piece of art, but also to enable you to enjoy the progress as you loop your way through the design.

***The Yarn*** - By now, you have decided on selecting the best punch needle that will help craft an elegant form of fabric art. The next most important item you want to choose is the yarn. Your yarn must match up with your choice of needle. A punch needle that has regular width requires a heavy rug yarn (3-ply) or a knitting yarn that is heavier than most other yarns. If you have a thinner yarn and are keen on using a regular punch needle, then the best thing to do is to double up or triple your yarn before it makes its way through your punching tool. The most lucrative aspect of punch needle embroidery is that it allows you to thread non-conventional yarn such as ribbon, twine, or even thin strips of fabric. When using fabric strips, go for a one-fourth inch (¼") width to achieve the best results with your punch needlecraft.

***Backing Fabric*** - A woven fabric that is not too stretchy is used as a backing material in punch needle embroidery. There are many types of backing fabric available in the market, and your choice will depend on the punch needle and yarn you already chose to complete your project. Backing fabric is also known as a foundation fabric. It is important to understand that a regular fabric may not be used for punch needle projects, and the needle tends to tear the fabric apart to make a big hole. The yarn will not be able to adhere to regular fabrics, and the fabric invariably gets damaged beyond repair.

In general, weaver's cloth is the material of choice for use with a small punch needle and embroidery floss. That makes sense as the weaver's cloth is a tightly woven fabric. Weaver's cloth is essentially a poly-cotton blend, and, therefore, is stronger and stretches less than pure cotton. The heaviness of the weaver's cloth is also ideal for securing loops from the punch needle and for holding them in place. In case you choose to go with the larger punching tool accompanied by heavy yarn, the fabrics that have a loose weave work best. A preferred fabric for the purpose is the monk's cloth, burlap, or rug warp.

Before starting your first project, there are four main options you want to consider when selecting the right fabric. We will consider the pros and cons of each of the four fabrics most suitable for punch needle embroidery - monk's cloth, burlap, linen, and rug warp.

**Monk's cloth** - The softest and most suitable fabric for punch needle embroidery is the monk's cloth. Most fabric artists prefer the monk's cloth to make their favorite purses, wall hangings, rugs, and pillows. It is also easy to sew after completing your project, as it is stiff and allows the needle to complete stitches with ease. Although the monk's cloth has strands that are close together for holding the yarn, there is still the right degree of gap in between strands to be able to correct errors during punch needle embroidery. When selecting your monk's cloth, ensure that you do not buy a variation that is used for working with other types of embroidery. The monk's cloth that is specifically meant for punch needle embroidery may be chosen for your project. However, you may not like it to show up as a background in your finished project. It works best when you plan to cover up the whole fabric with loops when carrying out your punch needle project.

The monk's cloth is created from 100% cotton and is a sturdy fabric. It also incorporates a high degree of flexibility. When designing bags, pillows, and stuffed toys, you may want to work with the monk's cloth as it imparts a certain degree of flexibility to the finished piece. Monk's cloth is also available in different types of weaves and sizes. The weave is a measurement of the number of holes per inch. A specific term, the "fabrics count," is used to describe the type of weave of the monk's cloth. For a typical project, you may want to settle for a 7-count or 12-count monk's cloth. The 12-count monk's cloth is generally preferred using the larger gauge needle. On the other hand, the 7-count cloth may not perform well as its weave is quite open, and the punch needle may not be able to hold the cloth together tightly.

**<u>Linen</u>** - Linen is another beautiful backing fabric for punch needle embroidery. Linen also works well when you have spaces in your motif and you would like fabric to show. Linen is a light material and has a luxurious finish. It is light-weight, yet sturdy, making it an ideal choice for punch needle embroidery projects. The uniformity of fibers in linen is somewhere in between rug warp and burlap. Fibers woven in burlap tend to be less uniform when compared to linen, but rug warp has considerably more uniform fibers than linen fibers.

The fabric works well with many different designs, and the feel of the fabric and its weaving makes it possible to complete even large projects in a fraction of the usual time frame. The projects also tend to be completed quickly as you may choose to allow parts of the fabric to show, and, thus, finish more pieces at the same time without heaving to fill the background with a suitable color yarn. However, even linen does not allow a smooth stitching experience as it is relatively stiff. Linen also holds the yarn loosely, and you may sometimes have to contemplate whether it scores better than monk's cloth given the high degree of tightness the latter offers for your embroidery projects.  It may also create resistance when trying to punch through the fabric. Nevertheless, the resistance characteristic may be safely ignored on account of the high-quality finish and smoothness linen offers.

Most crafts completed using punch needle embroidery have a monk's cloth or linen backing. Still, some artisans may choose to go with rug warp. Rug warp contains a certain degree of stiffness, and you may want to consider this characteristic before settling for rug warp. Rug warp also offers several advantages, including uniform rows for a smooth punching experience, and a sturdier backing to hold even heavy duty strands.

**Rug Warp** - A rug warp is often used when making projects that require a stiff and sturdy quality to the finished piece. You want to choose rug warp when making a bench cover or the cover for your stool. It provides the right tautness to securely fit or staple directly on the wood. Similar to the not-so-impressive background of the monk's cloth, rug warp also has a light background that may not impart the splendid look your work of art requires when it shows up in spaces between and around your motif. You want to cover the monk's cloth with yarn completely to achieve a colorful look. Sometimes your yarn may not stay on the warp cloth as well as it does on monk's cloth. When trying to stitch the fabric after finishing up with your embroidery, it takes a lot of patience since the needle may often get stuck or may not slide easily. Finally, it comes at a high cost despite several of its not-so-nice-to-have features.

**Burlap** - Burlap is essentially made from jute and is a low-cost fabric that offers less resistance when punching through it. Burlap also comes in many different colors and may be available in most stores. The only thing you may want to worry about when using burlap is its uneven weave. This poses a disadvantage since you may find it an arduous task to complete straight lines. The holes in the burlap may also vary in size, and creating loops with the yarn may become quite difficult. Besides, sewing through the fabric is not particularly simple as it is a stiff material.

Working with burlap may even get messy with strands falling off the fabric due to the uneven weave and stiffness. The basic imperfections in the weave may make your finished piece less durable as the burlap may not be able to hold the yarn well. Finally, it shrinks when wet, and, if you did not pre-wash it, your design may warp when you wash the artwork. As a final word, although burlap is abundantly available at low cost and there are a variety of fabrics to choose from, it is best to choose a fabric after carefully scrutinizing its characteristics, including weave and stiffness.

***Punch Needle Frame*** - A no-slip embroidery hoop is most suitable for punch needle rug hooking. The backing fabric retains the right tension when using a frame and provides a taut surface to work with. It keeps lines straight to achieve an impeccably finished piece of art. There are many different types of frames available for rug hooking, including the no-slip embroidery hoop, DIY carpet tack frame, Q-snap PVC frame, and gripper strip frame.

**<u>Wooden frames</u>** - To commence your punch needle project, you could simply settle for the traditional embroidery frame made from wood. The frame is familiar to most artisans and doesn't let the fabric slip or shift. You may also get a frame that has fabric pre-glued and serve as a good starting point, especially if you are a beginner and testing around to find the ideal pressure to apply when punching through. You want to focus on the core skill of punching without having to worry about keeping the fabric securely in place, and so, the wooden pre-glued frame is a good choice.

Aside from the familiarity with wooden embroidery frames, most individuals prefer the elegant golden look of the frame and enjoy completing their piece of art while adjusting traditionally styled brackets and screws. However, if you choose to go with a frame that does not have fabric pre-glued to it, then you may want to think twice. You will have to focus on your punch needle design as well as making sure the fabric does not come loose in the middle of your work.  Another important aspect of the wooden embroidery frame you shouldn't ignore before making a purchase is the quality of hoops and screws. These basic components affect the sturdiness of the embroidery hoop.

Finally, the cost varies widely from one brand to another. You may choose from a wide variety of wooden frames available in the market. Wooden frames come in different shapes, and you may choose one that works well with your proposed idea. For example, you could go for a rectangular wooden frame with the fabric glued to it and start working on a wall hanging. Another option you could consider in this case is to design your wooden frame if you have woodworking skills.

**Plastic frame** - The other option available in punch needle frames is the plastic frame, which also offers a no-slip base to complete your embroidery project. The plastic frame also holds the fabric securely, and you rarely need to readjust the fabric as you go along. The plastic fabric gives a significant stretch to the fabric and makes it taut. It can stretch it better than the wooden frames, even without requiring any gluing or stapling of the material to the frame. However, the plastic frames may sometimes cost more than the wooden frames. The frames are often preferred among beginners when they're first acquiring their skills.

**Carpet tack frame** - Carpet tack frames may be most suitable for making rugs as they provide a taut backing. These frames are available in different dimensions, from 10 inches to 20 inches in width and height, or even more. You may also be able to get rectangular frames in several different sizes. The carpet tack frame supports heavy-duty wool rug yarn, such as the 3-ply yarn. You may also be able to work with strips of fabrics. If you do plan to move the rug, then almost any yarn works well. However, consider choosing sturdy fibers when moving the rug; thin fibers tend to snag.

**Chapter Summary**

- Although the fundamental materials you would require for any needle punching project are the same, you want to choose the best combination that suits your pattern well.

- Choosing the Punch Needle

  - When choosing a punch needle size, consider whether you'd be working with ribbon, yarn, or floss.

  - Punch needles may be either regular size or the smaller (thin) size. You want to use the embroidery floss with the thin needle and rug yarn with the regular needle.

  - Punch needles may measure 1.3mm, 1.6mm, or 2.2mm. The threader typically measures around 18 cm, and the needle handle may be 11cm long and 1.5cm wide.

  - The adjustable punch needle can create loops of many different lengths, allows smooth piercing and retracting of the tool, and requires minimal rethreading.

  - The downside of the adjustable punch needle is its grip, as most people feel it does not extend across the hand, making the

punching maneuver inconvenient,
especially for elaborate projects. It also
requires a threader, which may be another
inconvenience.

- o The main advantages of the Oxford punch
  needle are its ergonomic design, easy
  threading, and sturdy construction. Its
  performance is comparable to the
  adjustable punch needle. However, it allows
  you to work with only a single size loop.

- o The Craftsman punch needle may
  sometimes be preferred due to its easy
  threading and built-in mechanism to create
  different sizes of loops. However, its
  complicated threading and locking system
  may put you off.

- o The ultra punch needle is great for projects
  that require thin yarn or floss and has an
  ergonomic design, and you can create
  different types of loops. However, the major
  limitation is you cannot use thick yarn.

- o When purchasing a needle, consider a few
  important factors to make the right
  decision: ability to create different-size
  loops, cost, sturdiness, performance,
  rhythmic pierce-and-retract motion, and
  ergonomic design.

- Selecting your yarn

    o   Yarns must match up with your selected
        needle.

    o   Yarns may be available in different sizes - 3-
        ply heavy rug yarn, thin yarn, or fabric
        strips.

    o   Yarn size must match up with the punch
        needle you selected as some needles are not
        designed to work with thick yarns.

- Identifying the right foundation fabric

    o   The most common choice of backing fabric
        is the weaver's cloth.

    o   Monk's cloth is a soft and sturdy fabric, easy
        to work with, and created from 100%
        cotton. It is flexible and forgiving.

    o   Linen features an elegant finish and is a
        light-weight fabric. Linen fibers are
        uniform. It offers resistance when punching
        but might be most suitable when you want
        to leave the background as-is without
        punching a background color yarn over it.

    o   Rug warp is a stiff fabric and may be used to
        create upholstery such as a bench or stool
        cover. It has an uneven weave, and your
        needle may sometimes get stuck. It also
        comes at a high cost.

- o Burlap is a jute fabric that offers less resistance, although it is uneven and slightly stiff. It does not cost much but may shrink on contact with water.

- Several frames are available in the market, including the traditional hoop, wooden frame, plastic frame, and carpet tack frame.

In the next chapter, you will quickly recollect how to work with the punch needle. You already learned the basic needle punching skills in Part I of the series entitled *Punch Needle for Beginners*. You may want to skim through the different sections of the next chapter or skip the chapter completely if you feel confident about using the punch needle.

# Chapter Three:
# Revisiting Basic Needle Punching Skills

As you may recollect from Part I of this series entitled, *Punch Needle for Beginners*, the basic steps to complete a needle punching pattern entails transferring the design to the fabric, threading the yarn, and punching the pattern to completion. As a quick reference, follow this description of fundamental needle punching skills to create a simple punch needle project.

***Transfer your design and mount your cloth***- The first step to starting your basic punch needle project is to transfer your chosen design on the selected fabric using a water-erasable marker or a pencil. You will need to trace the pattern on the "wrong side" of the fabric as the design loops are created on the reverse side. Fabric artists sometimes project an image with considerable detail to make a tidy piece of craft. In this case, you want to make sure you do not move the projector or your fabric all through your project. In many cases, this may not be possible as you want to constantly rotate the frame to get a good grip on the needle.

Alternatively, you could use a transfer paper to create a design replica on the fabric of your choice. An important consideration here is that the reverse side

of your needle punching project is the "right side."
Therefore, you want to transfer a flipped image onto
the fabric to get the right image on the other side.

***Attach the fabric to a frame*** - Once you are
satisfied with the transfer of your design on your
chosen fabric, stretch the fabric to create a taut
surface to work with. Stretch the fabric and attach it
securely to your chosen embroidery frame. You will
most probably settle with the no-slip frame as it is
versatile and imparts a good stretch to the material.

When using the wooden embroidery frame, there
are different ways to work with the one that has fabric
pre-glued and one that does not. To work well with
the wooden embroidery frame that has no glue, keep
shifting your fabric as you go on with the design. You
may need to readjust the fabric now and then. These
types of frames are suitable for projects that require
you to move the fabric to complete the design. These
include making the pillow or other items for
decorating your home. If you want to create a wall
hanging, then the pre-glued frame would work best.

When working with your custom-designed wood
frame, you enjoy flexibility, and you may be able to
craft the desired shape. Once you have the desired
shape, you may glue the fabric to the frame and start
working on your punch needlecraft. The only
consideration with do-it-yourself frames is to be able
to punch or glue the fabric well since this first step
determines the success of your project. Furthermore,

you may find it difficult to remove staples, which sometimes makes this option less popular.

Fixing the material onto the plastic frame is much like fixing it onto the wooden frame. You want to leave extra fabric around the piece to which you transferred the design. You may typically want to leave about two inches of the fabric all around to be able to secure it in the hoop. This helps to tighten the fabric. You want to pull the fabric at the basic clock positions, that is to say, the 12 o'clock position, then the 6 o'clock position, and then finally tighten the sides of the fabric by pulling it enough at the 3 o'clock and the 9 o'clock positions as well. Finally, pull the fabric gradually all around the loop till you achieve a taut base to work on.

***Thread the yarn*** - The first step is to thread your yarn through the needle. The punch needle contains a big enough "eye," and you should not find it difficult to thread the needle with your choice of yarn. The thread has to just go through the eye of the needle, traveling upwards until it reaches the slot in the handle of the needle. The thread comes out of the slot in the handle of the punch needle located at its other end, i.e., the top of the needle. For punch needle tools that require a threader, you want to pass the threader so that it reaches the top end of the punch needle. Then you want to pass the yarn or floss through the metal loop. Finally, pull out the threader and insert it in the eye of the needle. Now insert the floss and pull the threader to get the floss ready for punching.

***Start punching*** - The way to hold the punch needle is pretty much like you would hold any other pen or pencil. You want to hold it steady and start punching through the holes in your fabric. Leave a bit of thread on the back of the fabric as your reverse side is the correct side for your finished piece. As indicated previously, you do not need to have any knots as the fabric tension is sufficient to hold your embroidery in place. As you complete each stitch of the punch needle, a loop of yarn is created at the reverse side of your fabric. As you go forward, making more and more loops, they tend to arrange in your design pattern with a certain tension of the backing of your loops created on the fabric.

The desired embroidery containing loops is created on the reverse side from your perspective. Therefore, think about which side of the fabric you want to use to display your final piece of craft. The other side of the fabric facing you as you punch the loops looks somewhat similar to a hooked rug. The biggest advantage of punch needle art is that it allows you to display your embroidery both ways. You may choose to either display the side with loops or the side with hooks, whichever matches up with your preferences.

You can also change direction while punching, and to achieve this, you want to turn your needle when it is in its down position. Punching repeatedly creates the typical flat stitches on one side and loops on the other side. Keep punching and follow the lines and curves of the design you transferred to your fabric. If you want to work with a different color, you want to do the threading of the needle once again, the same way as described above, and start working on your piece of fabric art. Whenever there is a mistake, or if a certain stitch did not come out perfectly, you want to pull out the floss and move your fingers briskly over the surface of the fabric and line up the weaving before starting to punch over the same area once again. To finish up with your piece of artwork, simply leave a small piece of thread on the reverse side and trim it.

**Chapter Summary**

The steps you need to follow to complete a simple needle punching design are as follows:

- Transfer your design to the cloth using one of the many recommended methods - draw directly with a washable marker, project the design onto the fabric with a projector, or use transfer paper to get a design replica.

- Attach the fabric securely to a suitable frame - you want to use a no-slip frame, wooden frame, or adjustable frame, whichever serves your purpose and type of project.

- Thread the yarn -  Use a threader or thread the needle directly, depending on the needle punching tool you chose.

- Start punching - Hold the needle like a pen sturdily and start piercing downward in the fabric and then retracting to create loops of the desired size. Leave tails of yarn at its ends and trim them neatly to complete your pattern.

In the next chapter, you will learn more about different stitches you can try with needle punching. You will also be able to try out new stitches that resemble traditional embroidery.

# Chapter Four:
# In-depth understanding of stitches and spacing

Punch needle embroidery allows you to create 3D effects and drawings with just the needle, yarn, and backing fabric. Over time, your punch needle skills and imagination will continue to improve, and you will be able to make unique and advanced pieces of art for your home, business, or for display at an art exhibition.

Advanced punch needle skills will enable you to create both flat and 3D versions of your motifs. You may choose to play around with pom-poms, add glamour to your artwork with the velvet stitch, and combine different embroidery techniques to achieve a creative work of art. Learning different types of stitches allows you to choose between adding volume to your embroidery or letting it remain simple, defined by tidy loops. The basic know-how of creating different textures on the fabric of your choice is the first step to creating a wide variety of artwork, including geometric shapes, abstract designs, and other detailed art forms.

***Basic Stitches*** – You may want to start with four basic stitches to understand how the punch needle behaves, and then incorporate an appropriate effect in your work of art. Most fabric artists would experiment with several different stitches, including flat stitches, long and short stitches and loops, shags, and fringes to subdue or accent portions of their design. As a beginner, it is best to start working with the flat stitch, which is the most basic stitch. As you go along, experiment with the stitch and loops to understand how you may vary the loop sizes and obtain different types of effects and textures on the same fabric.

*Flat stitches* - The very basic stitch you are creating with your punch needle is the flat stitch. The flat stitch is created on the "reverse side" of your backing fabric as the "right side" contains the loops. To create your stitches, punch the needle down, pull it back, making sure you do not pull it quite far from the cloth. Pulling it too far may undo your last stitch. Keep punching, following the pattern you traced on your cloth. Make sure you punch equal length stitches to obtain a neat and tidy look. Changing direction is easy. All you have to do is line up the needle in the desired direction. You want to simply rotate the embroidery frame and start punching in a different direction. Keep punching this way, changing direction now and then, until you are done with the entire area.

To restate, these flat stitches are regarded as the "reverse side" of your artwork. You will still have loops on the "right side," and the size of your loops will depend entirely on your needle size (its height). Short needles create small loops, and long needles create bigger loops.

***Creative Effects with Loops*** - There are several ways you could use the loops on the "right side" of the fabric. Now that you know it is possible to easily vary the size of your loops by merely changing the size of your needle, the next step is to obtain different effects with loops when working with the punch needle.

**<u>The Shaggy Look</u>** – You could use backstitch to create uniformity with the loops. Further, to get a shaggy look like "pom-poms," you want to make long loops and snip off the top of the loop. You want to create this effect after you are done with a few stitches and have a decent area covered by loops. When you have more loops, and you snip them off, you get a thick shag.

**<u>The Fringe</u>** – To create a fringe for your punch needle project, start punching the flat stitch on the reverse side. When the punch needle comes out from the other side of the fabric, pull out the yarn using your finger to make an exaggerated loop. Keep going this way until you have covered a good number of rows, and created enough loops on the "right side" of your fabric. Snip off the tops of your loops and trim them to the desired length to achieve your fringe.

**<u>Long and Short Stitch with the Punch Needle</u>** – Fabric artists often try to incorporate the long and short stitch from traditional embroidery when working with the punch needle. To do a long and short stitch with a punch needle requires relatively less expertise and less floss for a given area. Sometimes, artists mix hand embroidery with punch needle stitches to achieve the desired effect they imagined at the beginning of their project. It's a good idea to use different techniques side-by-side as long as the finished artwork meets your expectations. Punch needle embroidery has endless possibilities and is easy to do, as well as a rhythmic and relaxing exercise.

Here is a basic implementation of the long and short stitch for your next project. It's up to you to choose the most appropriate materials as different combinations produce different effects. For your first project, use the weaver's cloth as it has a tight weave. You could set out with an ultra-thin punch needle with a lower setting to create small and neat loops. However, the larger punch needle on the monk's cloth would work equally well. The difference is only in terms of the kind of effect you achieve with the finished piece of art.

Punch ½ inch or ¾ inch stitches to fill the area. The stitches finally start looking like the long and short embroidery stitches. The long and short stitches are not done on the "right side" of the fabric. When working with your piece of art, fill up space with long and short stitches. This way, you are using the side of the fabric with the flat stitch. The "right side" with loops will have a lot of spacing between two consecutive loops.

That said, there are a few tips and tricks you may want to apply to your long and short stitch to make your final craft look tidy. First, start with a small stitch and continue punching stitches of equal length to complete neat lines of stitches. When you reach the end of a line, turn around your embroidery frame and start punching longer stitches just beside the first line you completed. On reaching the other end, complete another line of stitches, this time with the shorter ½ inch stitches you did in your very first step. Keep going this way until you have finished the whole area. If you are concerned about the loops coming off, add glue to the back of your fabric to secure your embroidery. Ensure you leave a bigger tail at the back to make it more secure.

**<u>French knots with the Punch Needle</u>** – It is possible to achieve the "French knot" look using your punch needle. If you want to make a "French knot" sort of stitch, start punching long stitches on the reverse side. When the punch needle comes out from the "right side" of the fabric, you want to pull out the loop a little to make it look like a French knot. For every stitch you make at the back of the fabric, there is a loop on the other side. Keep going this way to achieve a line of "French knots". The spacing between the "French knots" is the length of the stitch on the other side.

You want to make the loops on the "right side" relatively short to make sure they imitate a "French knot" closely. Another important piece of advice is about using glue to keep the loops in place on the reverse side. This ensures your "French knots" stay as you intended as the loops will not be able to come loose and pull off the knot.

**Chapter Summary**

- It is possible to create three-dimensional effects and textures with needle punching.

- The basic stitch you create with a punch needle on the "right" side is the flat stitch, and the one on the "wrong side" is the loop.

- The different types of effects you can create with your punch needle include the fringe, the shaggy look, long and short stitch, and French knots.

- You can obtain more creative artwork by understanding how the various textures and stitches turn out on each side of the fabric and then applying the desired look and feel.

In the next chapter, you will learn the basics of rug hooking, a closely related fabric art skill.

# Chapter Five:
# Rug Hooking Basics

Needle punching is very similar to rug hooking. When using the punch needle, you are punching loops downward, and the loops appear on the other side - the "right side." However, rug hooking requires you to pull loops upward while holding the yarn under the backing fabric. Although the loops appear similar, the techniques used to achieve the two types of fabric crafts are quite different.

The materials you would need for rug hooking projects include:

- Foundation fabric - The foundation or backing fabric you would use to do the rug hooking

- High-quality yarn - Your choice of yarn for the rug hooking project

- The rug hook - Basic tool you will need for your project

- Wooden frame to keep the yarn taut - Different frames suitable for rug hooking are discussed in detail below.

Note, however, that it is entirely possible to use the punch needle technique to create beautiful rugs. That said, here is a brief overview of the rug hooking technique. Rug hooking is done using a lap frame or floor frame. New frames generally cost a lot, even as much as a few thousand dollars. As a beginner, you probably should go for a used frame or one that is on sale to make the whole project affordable and enjoyable. You want to settle for a frame that costs as much as 30-35 dollars and minimize the shipping cost as well.

A lap frame is made from a solid square at the bottom that is placed flat and rests on your lap. Imagine a cube with a hollow and slanted top surface and hollow sides. The lap frame looks a lot like that. There is a solid square piece of wood at the bottom and a slanted and hollow square at the top, held in place by four standoffs (or wooden bars). The wooden bars join the four corners of the two squares. Two standoffs (the ones closest to you) are shorter than the ones on the opposite side (farther away from you). The longer standoffs attach the edges that are parallel to those with the shorter standoffs. This arrangement creates a slanted square at the top. It is hollow and consists of grippers on its four edges to secure the fabric in place. The slanted frame has an incline towards you and doesn't just secure the fabric but also provides an appropriate angle to work with. An angled frame is convenient to work with, but not all lap frames are angled.

The two tiers of the frame allow you to place your hand with the yarn underneath the rug while your other hand does the hooking. The two tiers of the lap frame provide enough space to perform the rug hooking with ease. The top tier of the frame (angled in this case) is covered with grippers or needles to create a taut surface for your fabric. The grippers work flawlessly and do not damage the fabric as you move it from side-to-side to complete your design. This is true for traditional wool yarn. However, it may not be the case with traditional sock yarn.

Another type of lap frame contains structural support at the bottom to allow it to rock from side-to-side, giving you more flexibility when working with your fabric. In the category of lap frames, you may also find a circular frame with two tiers. You may also be able to get fancy frames that may be placed directly on the floor. These frames are much more comfortable and ideal for hooking medium to large size rugs. Floor frames are also much more convenient when compared to lap frames, and they give you a better posture while you are working on your rug. Your choice of the frame is entirely dependent on the type of project you are working on and your personal preferences.

The way to get a taut surface for working with your chosen fabric is to stretch it enough so that it is held in place with the combs attached to the four sides of the frame. It is fine to press the fabric onto the grippers without worrying about damaging the weave. You want to simply lift off the fabric to shift it and start working in a different area.

When using a punch needle, you do not need two tiers as there is no need to place your hand underneath your fabric to feed the thread. The punch needle itself contains the mechanism to feed the thread. More information on threading the punch needle is discussed in Chapter Three that covers the basic walkthrough of using the punch needle. The most common type of frame used when needle punching is the wooden frame. Punch needle frames are also discussed with recommended materials in Chapter Two that deals with the materials required for punching.

When working with rugs, the tool used is quite different from the punch needle. In rug hooking, you may choose between the larger and flat hook or the thinner pencil-style hook to create your design. Similar to choosing a suitable needle punching material, you may also choose one that works well for your project based on the thickness of your yarn. Note that pulling thick yarn or a strip of cloth with a smaller rug hooking tool may not work well as it will rip the yarn when you try to pull it up using the hook.

If you want the needle punching effect for your rugs, then it is best to go with the standard-size punch needle. Experts recommend using the Amy Oxford punch needle for medium to large projects as working with a tiny punch needle would take up too much time. For smaller projects, you want to go with a tightly woven fabric like weaver's cloth, a tiny punch needle, and thin yarn, such as the one containing three strands. On the other hand, if you plan to go with a medium to large-sized project, then the standard-size punch needle with a well-spaced weave fabric such as linen is recommended. You may work with a thick and heavy-duty yarn in this case.

When working with strips, you want to consider if the chosen width is easy to pull hundreds or thousands of times through your fabric. A #8 primitive cut would be difficult to pull through a monk's cloth. However, if you want to go with a #5 primitive cut, then the strip is thin enough to pull through gracefully between the weave of the monk's cloth. The best part is that using an appropriate thickness yarn or cloth strip based on the spacing in the weave of the fabric does not stress your wrists or palms as you hook hundreds or even thousands of hooks. The #3 primitive cut is a very thin strip and may work with smaller hooks. Thin strips allow you to accomplish a shaded texture or add detail to your finished piece of art.

Here's a brief step-by-step process of rug hooking:

***Step 1: Get the Fabric*** – Your first step is to get the fabric of your choice to make the rug.

***Step 2: Fix the Fabric to the Frame*** – Now set up your fabric on the frame as discussed before in this chapter.

***Step 3: Hold the Yarn*** – To hold the yarn well and feed it to your fabric to create hooks, you should take the yarn and hold it between your index and middle finger. Then you want to leave a gap and hold it again between your thumb and ring finger. In other words, you want to hold the yarn between two points, and this part of the yarn is what you feed to the hook to pull it upward through the fabric.

***Step 4: Place your Hand under the Fabric*** – Put your hand underneath the fabric while holding it in the manner described.

***Step 5: Punch through the Rug with the Rug Hook*** – When piercing with the hook through your fabric the very first time, pull out a piece of your yarn, which you could call "the tail." This piece secures the rest of your design. Next, pierce again and pull out a loop from the yarn you are feeding with your other hand. You want to pull the loop up and pull it at an angle to make sure you do not undo the loops as you go along.

If you go with a punch needle to accomplish the same purpose, then start punching, knowing well that the design is created on the reverse side with the loops (the "right" side). As discussed earlier, you do not need to place your other hand underneath as needle punching is just done from the top. You want to rest the frame at an inclined position on a surface like a table, and then start punching.

***Step 6: Continue Hooking*** – You keep going this way, following the pattern you want to trace. If you are just beginning to rug hook, you want to try different yarns, fabrics, and hooking tools to get a hang of the different textures you may be able to achieve with rug hooking. You also want to experiment with different yarns and fabrics and both thick and thin punch needles to find out how it differs from rug hooking.

## Chapter Summary

- Rug hooking is all about feeding the yarn from the underside of the fabric and pulling the loops upward by piercing a rug hooking tool through the fabric.

- Rug hooking requires a different type of frame, a lap frame or floor frame that allows space between two tiers of the frame for free movement of the hand that feeds the yarn to the hooking tool.

- In rug hooking, you stretch the fabric to get a taut surface, the same way you would in needle punching.

- As with needle punching, rug hooking also requires you to pair the right hooking tool with a compatible yarn thickness.

- In rug hooking, you hold the yarn on the underside of the fabric and then pull the hooks to the surface, fixing the material to the frame, holding the yarn under the fabric, and pulling loops upwards using the rug hooking tool.

In the next chapter, you will learn to create a basic rug pattern using rug warp as the foundation fabric.

# Chapter Six:
# Creating a Basic Rug Pattern

This chapter covers an in-depth, step-by-step guide to create a pattern using the rug hooking skill. You may extend the skills learned in this chapter to blend different color yarns and complete any pattern for your favorite rug. The materials you will need for this project include:

- Foundation fabric - You will require rug warp as the foundation fabric for your project.

- Yarn - Choose colors according to your preference that match with the chosen pattern.

- Punch needle - A regular punch needle that you prefer.

- Frame - Choose a frame for the rug warp that is convenient.

- A pencil or washable pen - You will need a washable marker if you choose to draw the design. You may also choose to go for a pre-printed fabric. The different options are discussed in Step 2 below.

***Step 1***: Secure the foundation fabric in its frame – Stretch the rug warp on your frame and secure all sides to get a taut and sturdy surface.

***Step 2***: Draw your pattern on the fabric – You may get a pre-printed fabric that already has a design on it and start off with your projects. This proves convenient for most beginners. Alternatively, you could draw your design freehand while your rug warp is stretched on the frame. You want to draw the design with a durable water-proof ink such as a sharpie industrial marker. Sometimes, fabric artists prefer washable ink to get an ink-free surface with their work of art. However, the sharpie design is also covered well with yarn as you punch along. Most patterns are typically done in black color for clarity when following detailed lines and curves in the design.

***Step 3***: Thread your punch needle – The next step is to thread your punch needle. To thread your punch needle, which requires a threader, you want to push the threader from the hole of the needle hook (the scoop) and up through its handle. Then you want to put your yarn through the loop of the threader. The next step is to pull the threader out, so it comes back down, pulling the yarn with it through the needle hook. Then you want to insert the threader a second time through the needle hook in a direction perpendicular to the needle, pass the yarn through the threader loop, and pull the threader back, so the thread comes back through the hole in the hook (or scoop) of the punch needle. An explanation for threading the punch needle is included in Chapter Three, focusing on a basic walkthrough of using the punch needle.

***Step 4***: Complete the outline and the major parts
– Start making small stitches, punching all the way
around the outline. The underside of your rug warp is
the "right side" and will contain the loops that adorn
your finished rug. Keep working on the outline,
turning the needle so that the "scoop" faces the
direction where you want to continue punching. When
you are done with one color, hold the thread from the
underside, pull the needle up, and snip off the thread
with a scissor. You want to pull this tail to the
underside containing the loops.

If you have two or more colors in your outline,
keep threading your needle and progressing with your
design until you are done with the outline and major
sections. Some fabric artists prefer to fill parts of the
image along with the outline if they intend to use the
same color yarn in those sections. This is only a
matter of your personal choice, and you may either go
with the outline first, and filling and shading next, or
blend the two activities together.

***Step 5***: Fill the parts inside the pattern – To
complete your design, you want to continue with the
rug hooking tool until all sections of your rug are filled
with the desired colors. You may have already filled
parts of the design in the previous step. This step can
get rhythmic and relaxing as you fill up large sections
of your fabric. You want to leave a thread tail on the
"right side" each time you want to move to a different
section on the image so that the loops in a specific
area are secure and do not come off. Pulling a bit of

the yarn (the tail) when starting and stopping needle punching for a defined area is covered in the previous step (step 4).

**Step 6**: Change the yarn and complete the pattern – You are likely to work on this step alongside step 5 or even step 4 according to your convenience and personal choice. To complete the pattern with its different colors, you want to thread the punch needle using the desired color and start punching. You want to pay close attention to thread the needle properly, leave a tail when you start punching a specific area and when finishing the area, so that you may be sure the loops are uniform and will not come off at the slightest excuse. A detailed explanation of threading the needle is covered in Step 3 of this chapter. You might want to review step 5 as it will guide you on leaving tails in a tidy manner.

Steps 1 through 6 work with any pattern of your choice. These are the basic guidelines you want to follow to achieve a professional craft. When you are through with your complete pattern, your first rug is ready.

**Chapter Summary**

To create a simple pattern using  rug warp as the foundation fabric, follow the steps below:

- Attach the fabric to a frame for a sturdy surface.

- Draw your pattern freehand with a washable marker.

- Thread the needle with the yarn.

- Start hooking the outline and major sections.

- Fill the rest of the pattern, leaving tails of yarn on the underside.

- Change yarn and complete the pattern.

In the next chapter, you will learn how to make a welcome mat with basic rug hooking skills.

# Chapter Seven:
# Making a Rug Hook Welcome Mat

This chapter guides you through a step-by-step process to create a welcome mat. The materials you would require to create a welcome mat are:

- Foundation fabric - A suitable material for this project is burlap

- A rug hooking frame - You may choose to go with a frame according your preferences

- A rug hook - The tool you would require to complete your project

- Washable marker - You will need the washable marker to draw a freehand design on the foundation fabric

- Sewing needle and thread - You will need to fold in the edges and sew borders to finish the project

To make your first welcome mat, follow these nine easy steps.

**Step 1**: Secure your rug on the frame – You may go with burlap this time, just to get a feel of the material as you weave your welcome mat. Burlap is a good choice for most projects due to its affordability.

It is a natural material (jute) with an uneven weave. Your welcome mat does not need to have a lot of detail, and you could go with burlap, in spite of the not-so-straight lines of thread, as you will be incurring less cost on procuring the raw material. Burlap is also a little stiffer than the other backing fabrics, which imparts the right look and feel to the welcome mat. Bear in mind that burlap may not do very well when exposed to water repeatedly. It shrinks when soaked in water and may also disintegrate gradually over time. You want to consider this characteristic of the material before going with it. Most individuals would prefer burlap as its affordability scores more than all of its minuses.

Another important aspect of successfully weaving with burlap is to take care of its edges before starting out. Burlap is an uneven weave, and its edges tend to fray. You want to secure the edges before starting to stretch the fabric and punch through it. To do so, you could go with something as simple as a masking tape applied on both sides, along the four edges of your fabric piece. Another way to secure the burlap edges is to do a zig-zag stitch with a sewing machine all along the edges of the burlap.

***Step 2***: Draw the pattern on the rug – Your first step is to transfer the pattern to burlap. You may simply draw the image with a water-proof marker. Alternatively, if you have a projector, then you could project even a detailed image on the fabric without having to worry about the markings. Another way to transfer your pattern on the fabric is to use graphite paper. Transferring a design to the fabric is also discussed in Chapter Three, entailing the basic walkthrough of using the punch needle. Although the transfer techniques describe punch needling, the same information is applicable even to rug hooking.

There are important considerations about the way you draw your image on the burlap.  First, ensure that the size of the burlap is larger than your pattern, as the edges of your finished piece will have to be folded underneath. Second, when drawing freehand, you want to use a ruler to achieve a good straight line, or you could simply follow along the weave of the burlap and define the different proportions of your design. Third, your pattern must be defined by an outline as you want to fill the spaces between the pattern with yarn and also add an outline to your welcome mat.

***Step 3***: Start hooking over the outline – It's time to start hooking. As discussed in Chapter Five on the basics of rug hooking, you want to hold the hook on top of the burlap and place your other hand with the thread underneath the fabric. The way to hold the thread is described in the same chapter. Keep piercing the hook into a hole between the weaving and pulling the yarn out at an angle until you complete the outline. The loops may be any length, as much as you pull up the yarn. But a consistent look matters most, and it's a good idea to keep pulling in such a way that they are the same height eventually. This way, you want to complete the rest of the outline.

***Step 4***: Continue punching to fill the detail –
Next, you decide on the color that goes with the
different parts of the design and holds that color of
yarn underneath the fabric. You keep pulling the yarn
upward through the fabric to achieve neatly arranged
loops filling up the different sections of your design.
It's amazing to watch the different colors blend with
each other as you keep hooking the fabric and pulling
the loops up. In the end, you achieve a beautiful
texture with the same-sized loops.

***Step 5***: Punch the desired text – Now that you're
done with the outline and also have the rest of the
detail in place, complete the part with the text on it.
For a welcome mat, this makes the piece of craft stand
out and adds the right accent to an inviting and
hospitable environment. You want to go slowly and
hook the text neatly to get straight lines and perfect
colors for all letters. Depending on the design you
chose and the text that came with it, you may have to
outline the different letters or fill them by hooking the
right-color yarn if they are thick letters. Doing this
task with care helps you achieve a printed-text effect
for your welcome mat.

***Step 6***: Draw an outline for the overall pattern –
You are almost there. Now it's time to create an
outline for the overall pattern. You want to go slowly
all along the outline you drew in Step 2 and complete
edges by hooking loops to form an outline for your
piece of craft. An outline accents your piece of work
even more and is a must-have for welcome mats.

***Step 7***: Fill the background – The last step is to look for areas that did not have patterns and detail and tend to show the burlap underneath. Make sure you fill the entire area with loops. You want to look for these areas and choose a neutral color or a contrast color, whichever suits your design, to finish up by filling these sections.

***Step 8***: Remove the rug from the frame and fold the edges – Your welcome mat pattern is now ready. You may go ahead and carefully remove the rug from the frame. In this step, you also want to remove the masking tape from the edges as you will secure them in the next step.

***Step 9***: Sew borders with running stitches – In this step, you want to cut the burlap, so there is an equal border all around your pattern. Place your finished piece so that the backside is facing you and fold the edges two or three times to secure the edge. Thread yarn in a regular needle and sew all the edges using a running stitch. Select a yarn that is the same color as your background, so the stitches blend well and do not show up. Make sure you fold the corners well, so they're not bulky. You may want to do a triangular fold at the corner followed by the required folds for the next edge to get a neat corner and edge. To complete the running stitch, tie a knot with the yarn. If you are worried about the messy look at the back of your welcome, you could go ahead and attach a piece of felt to the back to get a neatly crafted piece of work.

**Chapter Summary**

To make a welcome mat using the rug hooking style, follow the steps indicated below:

- Secure burlap onto the frame.

- Draw your pattern or transfer it with transfer paper.

- Complete the outline.

- Make more hooks to fill in details in the pattern.

- Use the rug hooking technique to complete the text.

- Create an outline for the pattern.

- Make hooks to fill the remaining area of the background.

- Take the rug off the frame and fold the edges.

- Use a running stitch to finish the welcome mat.

In the next chapter, you will learn to create a landscape pattern using your rug hooking skills.

# Chapter Eight:
# Rug Hooking Landscape Pattern

By now, you have mastered the art of rug hooking. You finished your first few pieces hooking various types of fabrics. Now it's time to try a more intricate landscape pattern. To commence your very own landscape pattern, you will need:

- A foundation fabric for rug hooking - A suitable fabric you prefer among the recommended choices.

- Fine yarn (preferably size 2) - Since the project requires a lot of detail, a thin yarn works best. Choose colors according to your pattern.

- Rug Hooking tool - A basic hook you find convenient.

- Frame - A suitable frame for your rug hooking project.

- Washable Marker - You will need to draw the pattern on the foundation fabric. Alternatively, you may choose a pre-printed design to complete your pattern.

The steps required to complete a landscape pattern are indicated below:

***Step 1***: Draw your pattern on the fabric – You start your project exactly like the rug hooking projects you have accomplished so far, i.e. by transferring your design to the chosen material. If you choose to go with a pre-painted fabric that already has a landscape on it, then you may skip this step.

***Step 2***: Fit the fabric onto the frame – The next step is to hold the fabric taut and permanently attach it to the frame by stapling it. This project shows you how to do a landscape that you may use as a wall hanging. Although there are endless possibilities to make use of the landscape pattern (such as using it on cushion covers, purses, or home décor), this project shows the steps to make a landscape pattern framed on wood.

To secure your fabric on the wooden frame, fold each edge two times and press it against one of the edges of the wooden frame. Staple it at four to five different points along the edge of the frame so that it is secured well. Then turn your wooden frame with the fabric and follow the same stapling technique for the other three sides as well. When you are done, you should see a taut fabric attached to the wooden frame.

***Step 3***: Complete the outline – You want to first complete the outline drawing loops with your hooking tool to get the pattern correctly.

***Step 4***: Start filling the mid-ground in your landscape – Hold the size 2 wool yarn under the frame with one hand and start piercing the hook with the other hand, taking up one loop of yarn every time you pull back your hook upward. The best way to get started with a landscape is by first completing the mid-ground in the landscape.

**Step 5**: Stitch the yarn and do the landscape objects – You want to change the yarn and keep hooking to complete your landscape design. Remember to follow the best practices discussed in the previous chapters.

**Step 6**: Complete the background – In this step, you complete the rest of the design with hooks to fill the background for your landscape pattern.

**Step 7**: Add detail to achieve greater depth – You may choose to continue hooking in elements such as clouds for more depth for your landscape pattern. Look for areas that you would stand out with an outline or add an additional color yarn to enhance your image.

In conclusion, the landscape pattern is similar to the patterns covered in the previous chapters. However, you want to put your imagination to work to achieve that additional shading or highlighting with your rug hooking abilities. Also, note that you could also try punch needling to achieve a professional masterpiece.

## Chapter Summary

To make a landscape pattern, follow the steps indicated below:

- Transfer the pattern onto the fabric.

- Make the fabric taut by stretching it on a frame.

- Make loops with the hooking tool and complete the outline.

- Start filling the mid-ground.

- Keep working, changing the yarn as needed.

- Complete the background.

- Add detail for more depth.

In the next chapter, you will learn how to create a floral pattern with the rug hooking technique.

# Chapter Nine:
# Floral Pattern in Eight Easy Steps

Here's your next lesson with more delightful ways to create a floral pattern using the rug hooking technique. In this chapter, you will not only learn how to make a floral pattern, but also understand great new tips and tricks to make your design look like none other. The materials you would require to complete this project include:

- Backing fabric - A recommended fabric for this project is hessian/burlap.

- Wide strips (approx. 2 cm length) - You want to work with strips of yarn this time to achieve a different effect.

- Rug hooking tool - A basic hook will serve the purpose.

- Frame for rug hooking - This project requires an adjustable sew-on frame with side struts.

- Pencil or washable marker - You will need a pencil or washable marker to draw the pattern freehand on the foundation fabric.

- Scissors - This is generally required to cut out excess cloth or snip ends of the yarn.

The steps to follow are explained below:

***Step 1***: Prepare your backing fabric and secure it on the adjustable frame – In the first step, you want to start by preparing your fabric and making an outline for your pattern on your backing fabric. We choose burlap (also called hessian) for this project as it has a loose weave made from jute fibers and serves as an ideal base for the heavy yarn we plan to use for the floral pattern. It tends to allow any type of thick yarn or strips to pass easily through its weave.

A fun and easy way to straighten the edges of your backing fabric, and make an outline for your pattern, is to pull jute fibers out uniformly wherever required. You want to use the tip of your scissors to pull out a thread at one point, and then use your fingers to pull out the fiber completely. To make straight edges for your foundation fabric (burlap), cut along the gap you just created with a sharp scissor. Repeat this step for the other three edges to obtain straight edges and sharp corners all around.

Now you want to do an outline for your pattern in the same way. Leave about an inch from the edge of your burlap and choose any point. This is your starting point. Start pulling the jute string by using the tip of your scissor. This creates your first straight edge. You want to follow the same steps for all sides of your fabric to obtain a defined frame for your floral pattern. Draw a line all along the gap created from pulling the jute fibers with a marker to make it visible.

This serves as your pattern outline. Your floral pattern will cover the area inside this outline.

As you finish your outline, you may notice gaps between the edge of the fabric and the outline that were created as the jute string came off. As you will not be working on this area, you may wonder how to conceal the gaps. You need not worry about this as you are going to fold the edges in on the reverse side and sew them. Your finished piece will only contain the pattern inside the marker outline so that no burlap shows up.

Next, you want to make a pattern on your foundation fabric. Sketch the design on paper to get the detail right. A good idea to complete your design on burlap is to use chalk to make your markings. You want to use a sponge and do away with the markings that did not come out well. When you are happy with your final design, make your final outline with your black marker.

Now that your pattern is ready, it's time to attach your fabric to the frame. The adjustable carpet frame we will use here has four sides that must be attached one by one. This feature makes the frame adjustable for any sized foundation fabric. Secure your fabric so that it fits well on the frame. Two sides of the frame (the long sides) contain upholstery webbing that is pre-attached (either stapled or nailed onto the wood). Stitch the longer sides of your burlap to these two sides, attaching the carpet webbing and burlap edge-

to-edge. Be careful while stitching so that two sides
are exactly parallel and the distance between the two
edges is the same throughout. Otherwise, your final
rug may appear distorted. Taking care to sew the two
sides of the webbing with the edges of the fabric
ensures that your fabric looks like a perfect rectangle.

The good thing about using adjustable frames is
that the fabric need not stay stretched all along. You
may wind the fabric on one of the longer sides till you
achieve a comfortable width to work with. Then you
may stretch your working area by securing the frame
using the side struts. The other two sides are the side
struts. After attaching your foundation fabric to the
longer sides of the frame, insert the side struts into
the slots at the ends of the longer sides. The side
struts contain holes for pegs. There are a few holes at
each end of the side struts. Their holes are designed to
contain pegs. You want to push a peg at each end of
the side strut, so your foundation fabric stretches
uniformly. Once you have a taut surface, you want to
place it, so there is space underneath to feed the yarn,
and you can start hooking your floral design.

**Step 2**: Cut your wool strips – go with wool
blankets or old jumpers and recycle them to make
your home décor. You want to cut them to obtain the
right size strips. If you want to cut strips out of woven
fabric, you need sharp scissors to cut out long strips
measuring a centimeter in width. Keep going until you
finish up with the piece of fabric. However, if you
want to recycle knitted wool, such as a jumper, make

sure you cut the strips along the lines and not across them. You want to carefully cut out the one-centimeter strips following lines already contained in the knitted fabric. Remember that the fabrics may vary in thickness. To get a uniform effect for your final artwork, cut out a wide strip if the fabric is thin and make only narrow strips for thick fabrics. Neatly cut strips fare well when you are trying to make loops with your hooking tool.

**Step 3**: Start hooking with the darkest strips and fill the outer sections of the petals – Hold your hook like a pencil, so it extends between your index finger and thumb. When piercing the hook through your burlap, push it till the thicker portion reaches in between the weaving, making a big enough gap for the yarn to come through. If you turn your hand too much, you may pierce the hook at the wrong angle, and the hook may catch the jute fibers instead of coming back straight through the burlap.

Hold your other hand with the yarn and push your hook through the weave and pull out the end of the fabric strip you are holding with your other hand under the frame. Leave it on the top to start with. Then make the next hole, quite close, about two fibers away. Use the darkest color strips to complete the outer sections of the petals. When making the loops on the top with the hooking tool, make sure the loops are equal height for consistency. If you accidentally pull out too high a loop, it is still possible to pull the yarn from underneath until you get the same height.

But if your loop is too low, it may just fall back. As you reach the end of your strip (the yarn), pull the last bit on top. That way, you have two small segments of yarn on top of your burlap, the starting segment and the ending segment of the strip of yarn. Start with your next strip of yarn at the same hole where you pulled out the ending segment of the previous yarn. Keep hooking the yarn along straight lines, placing them close to each other.

**Step 3**: Continue filling the middle sections of the petals with a lighter shade – Continue hooking with a lighter color strip to fill the sections that are for the middle section of petals. Make them all uniform and leave the ends of the strip on top to be trimmed later.

**Step 4:** Finish the petals with the lightest color for their innermost portion – The last part of the flower is its innermost section. Continue with your hooking rhythm, choosing an even lighter shade for the perfect shaded look. By the end of this step, you are mostly done with your flower.

**Step 5**: Start hooking with a yellow color to fill portions with pollen – Finally, start hooking the center with a shade of yellow yarn to indicate pollen in the center of the flower.

**Step 6**: Cut uneven strips with a scissor and finish up – Once you have hooked the entire area of your rug, make it neat by trimming the ends you left at the top. The backing fabric holds all the strips and they do not fall off. However, ensure you do not trim the bits too deep. The bits near the periphery tend to fall off at a slant angle. To make sure these are not trimmed too short, slide your hand to push the bits from one side of the periphery and start trimming them to a uniform size. Pushing them towards the center before cutting ensures you obtain exactly the same height for the ends, irrespective of their location.

Your last step is to fold in the edges to the underside of the fabric and then sew it up neatly so that only the part you hooked shows from the front. To make a wall hanging out of your shaded flower pattern, sew a strip of cloth (the sleeve) to the top edge on its underside. Drill holes near the edges of a wooden batten (roughly the width of the sleeve), and place it right through it. Tie ends of twine through the two holes at the ends of the batten to make a wall hanging.

**Chapter Summary**

The steps needed to make a floral pattern on burlap are indicated below:

- Secure burlap on an adjustable frame.

- Cut strips of wool for the yarn.

- Start hooking using the darkest strips for the outermost sections of the petals.

- Use a lighter shade to create loops with a lighter shade of yarn for the middle sections of the petals.

- For the innermost section of the petals, use the lightest shade of yarn and continue hooking.

- Finish the pollen using yellow colored yarn.

- Trim the tails and finish by sewing the edges to the underside of the fabric.

In the next chapter, you will find a rug hooking and needle punching pattern gallery for more inspirational patterns.

# Chapter Ten:
# Needle Punching and Rug Hooking Gallery

Now that you have a certain level of expertise in rug hooking and needle punching skills, here's a carefully selected collection of patterns and designs you could use to recreate your very own artwork. The skills required to complete the patterns have already been covered in the previous chapters. If you are still unsure of what materials you would need for punch needling, then head straight to Chapter Two, which describes how to select the right materials in detail, including your punch needle, backing fabric, embroidery frame, and yarn. To recollect how to do a basic punch needle project, go to Chapter Three, and read your basic walkthrough of how to use the punch needle.

You may obtain more information on the different types of stitches you could use to make your punch needle project neat and professional from Chapter Four. The chapter covers, not only basic stitches such as the flat stitches, but also demonstrates how you could use different types of loops to make fringes and shags. Other stitches from traditional embroidery that you would replicate with the punch needle are the long and short stitch and French knots, which are covered in the same chapter.

If you would rather go with a rug hooking project, you may start with Chapter Five, focusing on rug hooking basics. You may find the materials required for your rug hooking project and the basic explanation of the unique technique of rug hooking in the same chapter. A basic rug hooking pattern is also explained in Chapter Six, which assumes you have a pattern with an outline and areas to fill up with yarn. That means you have already mastered the art of creating different effects and patterns by the end of the chapter. If you want to try out more basic patterns before you embark on one of the projects included in this gallery, then you may as well create your own welcome mat and landscape pattern described step-by-step in Chapters Seven and Eight, respectively.

That said, it's now time to choose your project and start rug hooking or needle punching, whichever technique suits you best!

# Chapter Eleven:
# How to use Needle Punching to Create a Grape Pattern

Punch needle embroidery works wonders with the grape pattern. It's an ideal choice since you get a soft texture to fill up spaces that show delectable grapes. In this chapter, we will create a grape pattern with purple grapes and fresh green leaves. We will then highlight some of the areas of our foundation fabric with a running stitch using a different color. The materials you would need to get started are:

- Foundation fabric (monk's cloth) - This project requires a tight weave fabric as thin yarn is selected for an intricate design.

- Yarn - You will need thin yarn in black, green, and two shades of purple.

- Ultra Punch needle - This project will help you learn an intricate design with the use of a thin yarn.

- Punch needle hoop (frame) - A regular embroidery frame is preferable.

- Pencil or washable marker - Draw the design on the foundation cloth before starting.

- Scissors - This is generally required to cut out excess cloth or snip ends of the yarn.

- Sewing needle - The design requires a little decorative running stitch.

- Black thread - The black thread is required to complete the running stitch.

When you have the materials ready, follow the steps to complete your grape pattern. A step-by-step guide is included below:

***Step 1: Secure the cloth on the hoop*** - You want to stretch your monk's cloth on a regular embroidery hoop to obtain a taut surface to work with your punch needle. Monk's cloth is suitable for this project since it has a tight weave and holds loops well as you punch your way through the pattern.

***Step 2: Draw the pattern on the cloth*** - The next step is to transfer the pattern on the cloth. We will use a pencil or washable marker to make sure the markings are not visible in your finished piece. You might want to recollect transfer techniques that may be ideal for your choice from the explanation available in Chapter Three, covering a basic walkthrough of the punch needle.

***Step 3: Thread the punch needle with a shade of purple*** - Take the dark purple or the light purple yarn and thread the punch needle. More information on threading the needle is covered in

Chapter Three on the basic walkthrough of the punch needle. After threading the needle, start with the outline for the grapes you plan to color in the selected shade, as elaborated in the next step.

**Step 4: Choose grapes randomly to outline and fill them** - Choose grapes you want to fill with the selected shade of purple and start punching the outline, followed by neat adjacent lines of loops to fill up the entire space contained in the grape. Keep working through the pattern until you have filled all grapes with the selected shade of purple. You should see gaps in your pattern by now that are supposed to contain the other shade of purple.

**Step 5: Fill the remaining grapes with the other shade of purple** - Thread your punch needle with the other shade of purple and work your way through the outlines for the rest of the grapes, followed by adjacent lines of loops to create the filling inside the grapes. When you have completed this part of the pattern, all your grapes should contain a shade of purple, either the dark purple shade or the light purple shade.

**Step 6: Complete the leaves with the green yarn** - Switch the green yarn and complete the leaves in the pattern with it. Align neat lines of loops side-by-side to complete one leaf, and then move to the other leaf. Keep going this way, slowly and steadily, until you have all leaves covered in soft and shiny loops of yarn.

***Step 7: Continue punching with the black yarn for the stick*** - You are almost finishing up with your design, and the last part of the punching process is to complete the stalk. Thread the black yarn for the purpose and start punching the stalk. Follow the same technique you have been using all through and complete the loops for the stalk. This step finalizes your punching activity.

***Step 8: Create the dotted line*** - The dotted line adds a certain highlight to your overall pattern. Take a regular needle and use a black thread to complete the dotted line with a running stitch. A running stitch is a familiar way to create a dashed line. You want to thread the regular needle, passing the thread through it and doubling it up. Make a knot with both ends of the thread. Then, pierce the needle from the underside of the fabric, so the knot also remains on the underside. At this point, you should have the needle with its length of thread on the top of your fabric.

Now, pierce the needle from the top downwards, so the needle emerges from the underside, making a stitch on the top of the fabric. Leave the same distance and pierce the needle from the underside, so it comes out with the thread from the top. Repeat these two steps to create dashes. When you create dashes at the top of the material, a line of dashes is also created on the underside of the fabric. When you are happy with your dashed line, pierce the needle downwards from the top of the material, so that it emerges from the bottom. Make a knot supporting it with an adjacent stitch as you would for any other regular embroidery pattern.

Your pattern is now good to go, and you could secure the edges to fit it as a cushion, wall hanging, or any other home decor as you may feel appropriate.

**Chapter Summary**

Follow the steps below to create a grape pattern by needle punching:

- Secure monk's cloth on the embroidery hoop.

- Draw your grape pattern with a pencil or washable marker.

- Use one of the shades of purple and thread your ultra-thin punch needle.

- Outline grapes randomly and fill them with the selected purple shade.

- Use another shade of purple to finish the remaining grapes.

- Fill the leaves using green yarn.

- Continue punching and complete the stick with black yarn.

- Add a dotted line with a regular running stitch.

In the next chapter, you will learn about popular techniques to finish needle punching projects.

# Chapter Twelve:
# How to Finish your Needle Punching Projects

You have created some great punch needle projects so far. They may be elaborate pieces of artistic excellence or simple embroidery patterns. If you are worrying about how to finish them up for an elegant piece of home decor or item for sale, here are a few possible ways to utilize your punch needle patterns in creative ways.

***Pillows*** - A great way to use your punch needling masterpiece is to sew it on a pillow cover, so it adds color and style to your pillow. Punch needle craft is great for pillows as it gives a soft feel and looks fine with most upholstery.

***Frames*** - Frame your punch needle project and hang it on the wall, rest it on a side table, or display it in any place you feel is appropriate. You might want to contemplate which material, color, and pattern you want to use to make sure your design matches up with the frame. Most individuals would choose a frame that accentuates the punch needle design. Using a frame that is too loud in terms of its color or pattern may subdue your embroidery pattern. In general, solid colors that contrast or blend well with the design work well in most cases. Another great idea to add a professional touch to your project is to find a wool mat in a color that goes well with your work and attach it to your punch needle project. You may sew it on the underside to get a great background for your finished artwork.

***Attaching to a wooden hornbook*** - Wooden hornbooks are recommended for embroidery projects. They work well with punch needle projects, and their available sizes and shapes allow you to pick a suitable backing for your project. You may also get a hornbook done by your local woodworker. The made-to-order backing may prove much more useful than a ready-made one.

***Stand-alone project*** - One of the most impressive ways to display your punch needle pattern is by making a stand-by-itself figure out of it. You could add some real accessories to make it look even better. You should plan ahead if you want to add accessories to your final 3D figure. This is an essential step as you want to resize your pattern to the correct proportion with respect to the accessories you already purchased. Imagine the finished piece, get the right accessories, and then print your pattern accordingly to start punching it.

When you have finished punching your pattern, cut around the pattern, leaving about an inch of the fabric all around. Fold the fabric to the backside of the pattern. Now cut out a piece of felt wool to fit the back of the pattern. The backing must be exactly the same size and shape as the original pattern. When you have the piece of felt wool ready, sew it onto the pattern, but leave the bottom open for stuffing. Now, sew on a felt wool base that fits the gap between the punch needle pattern and felt wool backing. Sew all around to just leave a small gap for the soft pellets that will go in as stuffing for your stand-alone figure. Fill the figure with these pellets and sew the remaining edge to seal your figure. Your stand-alone figure is now ready, and you may display it on any counter or tabletop.

*Clothing* - Another fun way to use your needle punching pattern is to stitch it onto your favorite shirt. Punch needle patterns look great with denim and may also work well in the form of skirt borders, sleeve patterns, and as far as you can possibly imagine.

*Pin* - Another way to revamp the look of your old coat is to make a pin for it so you may wear it any time. First, make your needle punching pattern, complete with a design and a background for it. Cut the foundation fabric around the design, leaving about one-fourth of an inch all around it. Turn the fabric over and press it onto the underside of your pattern. Turn the pattern back again, and you should no longer see any of the backing fabric. Next, cut out backing from felt wool by placing the pin on the wool and making a chalk mark all around it. Sew the felt wool with your pattern, their wrong sides together. Finally, sew the pin to the backing of felt wool, and your pin is ready.

***Stocking*** - To make a punch needle stocking, place the felt wool on top of the punch needle pattern and sew it on with a zipper foot. Leave the top of the stocking open. Trim the edges of the felt wool, about ¼ inch all around the stitched lines. Leave a little more length of felt wool at the top (about ½ inch). Turn it over and press. The fabric that was left at the top of the stocking goes inside. To make your lining, trace the outline of the stocking on tracing paper and cut it out. Fold the cotton lining, so that the right sides are together, and trace the pattern onto the lining. Sew along the line you just traced but leave the top open when you are done, and trim the edges, leaving ¼ inch all around the lines you just stitched. The extra fabric for the lining is pressed on the outside. When you have the lining ready, place it inside the stocking. Finally, stitch the lining to the stocking all along the top.

***Ornaments*** - You may wonder how the punch needle craft may be used to create ornaments, but it is quite possible to do so. Punch needle ornaments don't need backgrounds, and you could create a large number of projects in a fraction of time. To make a punch needle ornament, cut a piece of felt wool the same shape and size as your punch needle pattern. Cut a thin piece of cardboard the same shape as your pattern but about ¼ inch smaller than it.

You want to trim the foundation fabric of your punch needle pattern so that about ½ inch of the fabric is left all around it. Press the edges of the foundation fabric to the back of your punch needle pattern. Now, place the wool backing on the backside of the pattern and start sewing them together with a matching thread. Stitch the excess foundation fabric and the wool together, making sure no loops are sewn into the edge.

When you have stitched the pieces halfway through, fold an 8" ribbon with jute fiber, or any other string, and insert it in the space between the two fabrics. Continue stitching to secure the ribbon in place. Also, slide the piece of cardboard in between the two fabrics and continue stitching to finish your ornament.

*Basket* - The best thing you could do with your punch needle project is to use it to decorate your home. You could attach it to a sleeve that wraps around your basket. Punch needle patterns are soothing to the five senses and also safe for children. So you may use the wrapped basket anywhere, such as your home or office.

*Hanging* - It's quite easy to make a hanging out of your punch needle pattern. All you have to do is sew on a backcloth and a ribbon to hang it.

*Tree skirt* - Punch needle patterns also look great as tree skirts. They impart an elegant look to the tree skirt, and designing them is easy. All you need to do is stitch the punch needle patterns to the tree skirt in an impressive layout.

***Three-dimensional project*** - Another unique way to use your punch needle pattern is to create a 3D project. The technique you would use to create the 3D figure is quite similar to the stand-alone project described earlier in this chapter. You want to understand how the different parts of your 3D figure attach together to make the final piece.

As an example, if you want to make a vegetable man, you are most likely to stuff the vegetable, which is a punch needle pattern. The vegetable pattern may represent the face and body of your vegetable man. Your next step would be to stuff the hands and legs of your vegetable man and sew them to the body. Whether you want to needle punch just the head or the hands and body as well, is a matter of personal choice. Whichever way you choose, stuff all parts of the vegetable man and sew them up before attaching them neatly in the right places.

***Tea towel*** - Punch needle craft adds glamor to your kitchen. If you are tired of looking at the checkered and striped patterns all around you, then it's time to add some fun aspects to towels and mats. Now that you have a good idea about working with the different types of fabrics, you could start needle punching directly on a kitchen fabric such as a tea towel to make it a decorative piece.

***Table Mats and Coasters*** - Create your table mats and coasters in a way similar to most other projects discussed here. All that they need is a backing to go with the design, and you are good to go.

**Chapter Summary**

There are several ways to finish needle punching patterns you created:

- Sew onto pillow covers.

- Attach your pattern to a wooden hornbook.

- Make a stand-alone project.

- Stitch it onto your clothing or make a coat pin.

- Make stockings for winter.

- Make decorative ornaments.

- Make basket sleeves, handings, or tree skirts.

- Convert the needle punching pattern to a 3D project.

- Needle punch on a kitchen towel to enhance its look.

- Make table mats and coasters.

In the next chapter, you will learn a simple technique to dye your own wool.

# Chapter Thirteen: Dyeing your Own Yarn

One of the best things you can do to make your needle punching projects even more interesting and fun is to dye your own yarn! Getting to know the right technique to do this helps you achieve stunning colors at a low cost. A tried and tested do-it-yourself method for dyeing yarn gives you the ability to obtain a color you prefer for a specific project. Once you feel confident about dyeing your yarn at home, you may well complete many more beautiful projects.

There are typically three materials drawn into yarns: wool, cotton, and acrylic. The following steps describe a standard process for all three types of yarn. The materials you would need to dye the yarn include:

- Microwave-safe container - To dye the fabric well, the solution is heated in a microwave.

- Yarn - You want to try how different types of yarn absorb the dye. We will work with wool, acrylic, and cotton to see what happens.

- Water - You will need to soak the yarn in water for it to uptake the dye.

- Vinegar - The vinegar is added to enhance the color.

- Fork - You will require a fork to lift the fabric from the hot dyeing solution.

Here are the steps you want to follow:

***Step 1: Let the yarn soak in water*** – Your first step is to soak the yarn in water. Use a microwave-safe bowl to hold the water as you'll be heating the container later on. Fold the yarn several times to make it compact and tie it somewhere across the center. Put this neatly folded yarn in the container filled with water and let it soak for at least fifteen minutes before proceeding to the next step.

***Step 2: Prepare a dyeing solution*** – Add vinegar and color to the water container. Let the color dissolve completely. Food color is also a good coloring agent and gives the basic shades you mostly need for most projects.

***Step 3: Apply heat to the solution*** – Heat the container with the dyeing solution and yarn in a microwave till the water starts boiling. The heat enables the yarn to take up the color dissolved in the solution. Remove the bowl from the microwave when you see that it has heated enough, in other words, when it begins to boil.

***Step 4: Remove the yarn on cooling*** – Allow the solution to cool and remove the yarn, preferably with a fork or spoon, to prevent your hands from accidentally scalding. Sometimes, the water can be very hot even after some time has passed. Remove the dyed yarn from the water and place it in a tray.

***Step 5: Wash the yarn with cold water*** – Wash the yarn with cold running water. Different types of yarn take up a different quantity of color. You will notice acrylic did not take up any color, cotton takes up a little color, maybe 50%, and wool takes up the most color and gets dyed to a very dark shade.

***Step 6: Set the yarn to dry*** – The last step is to allow the yarn to dry. On drying, the final color of the yarn may change. The color generally tends to lighten a bit. However, you will find that wool takes on a bright and uniform color after drying, while cotton lightens further, taking up a much lighter shade compared to wool. Finally, acrylic does not take up any color at all, as you observed on washing with cold water.

Wool is generally the yarn of choice for most fabric artists, and wool is easy to color at home with simple tools and straightforward technique. Using this technique, it is possible to obtain your preferred color, even for large quantities of yarn.

**Chapter Summary**

To dye your own yarn, follow the steps below.

- Soak the yarn in a microwave-safe container for about 15 minutes.

- Add vinegar and dye to the water.

- Transfer the bowl to a microwave and heat until it reaches a boiling temperature.

- Let cool and transfer the yarn to a tray using a fork.

- Wash with cold water until you remove all excess dye.

- Let the yarn dry.

In the next chapter, you will learn how to make money from your needle punching and rug hooking skills.

# Chapter Fourteen: Making Bucks

By now, you must have learned many useful skills while working on the exciting needle punching and rug hooking projects covered in this book. One of the best ways to utilize these skills is to set up an online store and start selling your artwork.

This chapter serves as a guide to help you accomplish your first few steps towards opening your store. You will find tips on how to strategically launch a successful business and important resources you may utilize to start and run your business.

It's best to follow a step-by-step process described below.

**Step 1**:  Understand how to set up a shop at Etsy – Etsy is a top platform for all kinds of handicrafts and is most suitable for your needle punching and rug hooking projects. You have the maximum chance of achieving a constant stream of orders from interested customers.

Etsy supports craft enthusiasts from all walks of life. You will find many shop owners and small businesses offering rare and hand-crafted items. Prior to opening your shop, it's best to understand their seller policies and the fee involved. Etsy features separate policies for its buyers, sellers, and third-parties.

In addition, participants are also bound by its terms of use and must comply with its privacy policy. As a seller, it's important to understand how to conduct your business online, acceptable behavior, policy on taking part in community settings, terms related to advertising and marketing your merchandise, the nature of payments, and the fees Etsy charges for its services.

It also contains guidelines on what to sell in the form of handmade items and restricted items and responsibilities related to the delivery of items sold. To be able to scale your business in due course of time, it is best to understand Etsy policies describing seller referral and seller protection. They're quite relevant when you first start pursuing your business goals.

Another important area to familiarize yourself with is Etsy's terms of use. Every seller is expected to agree with the terms of use at Etsy, and it's best to be aware of them before committing to their policies. The broad areas addressed in Etsy's "Terms of Use" include dispute resolution, privacy, advertising, guidelines for opening and maintaining an Etsy account, and content posted on your seller page with relevant permissions and responsibilities.

Etsy also outlines rights that you grant, such as those related to distribution, reproduction, publicity, and the like. It contains precise guidelines to report inappropriate or unauthorized content. Finally, it outlines do's and don'ts, termination policy, conditions for various warranties, indemnification clauses, and contact information.

***Step 2***: Open your Shop on Etsy – To open your shop, create your account. Etsy offers free registration on a review of its terms of use and privacy policy. To register with the website, fill their form in, and confirm your email address. On confirming your email address, you are ready to start selling. Click on the "Sign In" link at the top of the page and sign in to your account. Etsy allows you to sell your handicrafts, as well as buy from other sellers, through a single account. A good practice is to fill in your profile with all the required information. Your profile picture is an essential part of a good business appearance.

The next thing you want to do is start selling on Etsy. Although you do not require a business license to sell there, you are expected to follow the laws that are applicable to small businesses. To become a seller on Etsy, click the link "Sell on Etsy." You will find this link in the footers section. The second column reads "Sell" and contains a few relevant links for sellers and affiliates; click this link to start selling.

The landing page for new sellers contains significant information about the different value-added features offered by Etsy, including its low listing fee, commission, PayPal processing fee, and payment requested for advertising. It also describes tools for promoting and managing your selling operations and advertising, accepting payments, applying analytics, and seeking support services.

Etsy offers two types of membership packages: the standard package allows you to set up your store without any additional fee charged on a monthly basis. The "plus" package is priced at $10 per month and provides additional tools to expand your business and achieve a higher degree of growth. On subscribing to the "Plus" package, you'll gain access to several customization options to enhance the look and feel of your website, and that will help direct customers to your website. The package also supports inventory management. This allows you to send mail to customers who have requested a specific inventory item that is not currently available. It also enables you to keep track of popular items, so you can plan which items to add to your inventory. Finally, members participating in the "plus" package get rewarded with additional credits to list additional items and advertise their wares.

If you feel stuck anywhere while setting up your store, Etsy offers an excellent support system you can use to resolve your precise issue. It is possible to seek support over the phone or email, and in community spaces by interacting with other sellers. The company also distributes a newsletter regularly with helpful advice for sellers and offers tips for running a successful business.

***Step 3***: Finishing your Shop Setup – Setting up your shop on Etsy is one of the most vital aspects of your online business. Make sure you have a proper workflow in place to be able to  complete orders on receiving inquiries. Plan ahead and document the necessary aspects of your production cycle, general business and selling policies, and the shipping method. That will enable you to fill in the right information in the right place and become a popular seller in no time.

There are a few things you need to make sure you have ready as soon as you register. The first thing to do is to create an impressive logo and banner and upload clear and high-resolution pictures to ensure your brand creates the right impression in the minds of your readers. Once you are happy with the way your banner and logo appear, send your very first communication to prospective buyers. That helps them know your products will be available shortly.

Another important aspect of your shop that most sellers tend to ignore is the "about" section. This is one of the most important sections of your online store, and you want to communicate the most impressive aspects of your business with the help of a blend of pictures, text, and videos. Your "About" section is the place where you describe your philosophy, why you chose to open your store, and interesting aspects of your business offering.

Lastly, it is crucial to understand and establish communication policies with the members of your team and other people working with you. You also want to formally specify your policies related to payments, return and exchange of items, general guidelines, and shipping. This serves as a good information base, not just to keep your buyers informed, but also to straighten things out in the case of a dispute.

***Step 4***: Adding listings to your Shop – You're all set. The next step is to start listing your products. Simply click on the icon that represents your account and then click on "shop manager." Thereafter, click "Listings" and the "add a listing" link. This opens your product page, and you have the opportunity to list your product with all relevant information. Add photos and videos of your product, a thumbnail image, and other details and description. This page also captures information about your method of shipping, marketing, product price, and inventory. Make sure all this information is available before you proceed to add your product to the Etsy store. When you are satisfied with the information, click on "publish" to make your shop live on the storefront, or save the information you supplied by clicking on the "save your listing" button.

***Step 5***: Marketing, Branding, and Promotion – As an online seller, it is vital to find new customers and retain existing ones. You can take care of these aspects through your marketing strategy. Good online marketing includes several aspects, such as optimizing your store for efficient web search engines. The Internet has opened up several channels for sales and marketing for interested sellers. The most effective methods include using paid advertising to make your store popular, and marketing through social media accounts. Sellers can also use coupons to attract new customers or become part of a network of sellers to achieve a decent sales volume.

Etsy provides ways to set up and manage advertisement campaigns. Advertisements are displayed on different pages based on their website algorithm. By subscribing to Etsy Ads, your products start getting more exposure as they appear on the search results page and other internal pages that may provide a competitive advantage. These pages may be Etsy's "Market pages" or "Category pages." Advertisements are also visible in their mobile app. You have the option to set up a budget for the advertisement campaign and select the different products you want to list on the page.

Etsy ads can be set up and managed by clicking on the icon linked to your account and then clicking "shop manager." Now click "marketing" and then click on "advertising." In this section, you want to set up your budget per day. Etsy takes this as the maximum amount that may be spent on your items listed on Etsy. A minimum of one dollar may be set up as your budget on a daily basis. It is also possible to change your budget at any time. Once you have finalized your budget, it's time to start selling on Etsy. As your advertisements are displayed throughout the website, you get the opportunity to access Etsy insights to decide on the best way to get to the next level. Analytics available through Etsy allow you to explore new markets or expand your reach in existing markets.

Your shop is now ready, and your business and seller policies are all in place. Make sure you review your policies, product listings, and marketing, shipping, and payment methods regularly to achieve success in the long run. Besides Etsy, there are several other online platforms you want to explore. The most popular and relevant platforms are Freelancer.com and Fiverr.com.

Create and publish a complete profile on these platforms and start listing your products. Publishing your profile on multiple platforms allows your products to gain more exposure and gives you a competitive edge. If you choose to engage with multiple outlets, be sure you understand the terms and policies applicable to seller activity. Needless to say, being able to maintain your store in an organized way on many different online platforms is a huge step to becoming a successful online seller.

**Chapter Summary**

- Etsy is a leading platform to set up your online store for selling handicrafts.

- Etsy provides interesting options for advertising and marketing your products.

- Other relevant platforms include Freelancer.com and Fiverr.

# Final Words

Learning to be a professional in punch needle embroidery is both satisfying and rewarding. Unlike traditional needle and thread embroidery that most people find cumbersome, punch needle embroidery is one of the simplest forms of embroidery there is. Its simplicity allows you to create large masterpieces to enhance your home decor.

You can even create a high volume of embroidered pieces to sustain a business. All you need is a few basic materials, learn some standard best practices, and stay away from known pitfalls. When you have creative acumen, punch needle embroidery is the best way to turn a simple and plain fabric into an elegant and attractive piece of art.